ENERGY TO

ENERGY TO THRIVE

Journal for Mapping Your Path to Wholeness

Katie Dean, PhD.

BEYOND
BELIEF
—PUBLISHING—
YOU HOLD THE FUTURE IN YOUR HANDS

This material had been written and published solely for educational purposes. The author and the publisher shall have neither liability nor responsibility to any person or entity with respect to any loss, damage, or injury caused or alleged to be caused directly or indirectly by the information contained in this book.

The author of this book does not dispense medical advice or prescribe the use of any technique as a form of treatment for physical, emotional, or medical problems without the advice of a physician, either directly or indirectly. The intent of the author is only to offer information of a general nature to help you in your quest for wellbeing. In the event you use any of the information in this book for yourself or others, which is your constitutional right, the author and the publisher assume no responsibility for your actions.

Statements made in this book have not been evaluated by the Food and Drug Administration. This book and its contents are not intended to diagnose, treat, or cure any infection, injury, or illness, or prevent any disease. Results vary and each person's experience is unique.

ISBN: 978-1-957972-21-3

Table of Contents

Introduction

This journal accompanies the book *Finding the Energy to Thrive*. It is designed to allow you to explore your personal experience of living with chronic fatigue syndrome (CFS) and support you in building a roadmap to recovery. I collapsed in late 2002 and was diagnosed with CFS six months later. It took me twenty years to regain my energy and led me to explore some fascinating paths on that journey. I now look back on that experience as one of the greatest gifts of my life. I didn't simply return to the "old me" when I recovered: my journey led me to discover that I have more energy and more personal power than I had ever realised. For me, this was truly a return to wholeness, and that has opened up a life in which I am thriving, not merely surviving.

I intend for you to manifest the same miracle, and I appreciate that your journey and your experience will be different from mine. I have shared my experience and learnings in *Finding the Energy to Thrive*, inviting you, as the reader, to answer some journaling prompts that will support your own reconnection to Self, wholeness, and sustainable energy. This journal offers you the space to respond to those prompts. I have laid it out to correspond to the chapters in the book. So, you will see reminders of the main points covered in each chapter, followed by the journaling prompts. In order to get the maximum benefit, I recommend using the journal alongside the book. The book chapters expand upon the bullet points included here, providing you with examples and additional information to help you understand concepts that may feel new, perhaps even challenging. The journaling prompts also relate directly to the full information shared in the book chapters. Those questions are designed to help you gain awareness of how you are perceiving your experience and the beliefs you hold about CFS and your ability to recover. They will also assist you in understanding more about why your symptoms are occurring and what those symptoms are trying to tell you. Once you have that knowledge, you will be empowered to seek out treatments that can support your recovery. The process of recovery is a journey in itself, and this journal will also support you on that journey, helping you to see your inner world and connect back to your true Self in ways that are compassionate, loving, and supportive.

These pages are yours to use in whatever way you find helpful. They provide a safe space to confide your deepest fears and doubts, as well as to fill with your hopes and dreams. Please be as open and honest, raw and vulnerable as you can when you complete these pages. We are often taught that the secret to recovery lies in finding the "right" pill, practitioner, or protocol to bring that recovery. In my experience, those pills, practitioners, and protocols are simply tools that support us. The true path to recovery lies inside each of us. This may sound daunting, especially if you have already been seeking recovery for many years. Yet, it is very empowering. When you recognise you have everything you need already inside you, you also recognise your recovery is not dependent on finances, doctors, research, or any of the other external factors that may be out of reach for you. Instead, by tuning in to your true Self and uncovering the awareness of the power inside you, you will step onto your optimal, personal recovery path.

There is no judgement here, only love and compassion. No matter the shape or length of your journey, I invite you to seek the joy in each moment, to witness the pain with compassion, and to trust that you are on exactly the right path for your Soul. I know that you will reach the perfect destination for you, and this journal is here to support you on that journey. So, carry it with you, keep it close to your heart, and allow it to grow and expand as you also grow and move forwards.

With love and blessings,

Katie x

Chapter 1

Meet Your Guide

This chapter of *Finding the Energy to Thrive* focuses very much on me and my story. Yet, I wrote the book with the intention of supporting you. So, I would like to now invite you to begin a practice that we will be using at the end of each chapter. This is about turning the focus back on you and encouraging you to determine what you think, feel, and need. All of that is going to become the foundation for planning your road map out of the maze of CFS. We are often raised with the belief that healing comes from outside ourselves, through the medium of someone else qualified in understanding health. Yet, that person – or institution – is never actually healing you. They simply provide support in the form of information or possibly some kind of protocol. This creates a supportive environment in which your body can follow its innate healing path. Believe it or not, your body is already doing its best to bring you back to a balanced place of health. There may just be a few areas where it isn't receiving the support it needs. Some of those areas will require assistance from other qualified professionals. Other areas are things you can put in place, starting right now and requiring no external intervention. These elements are already within you, and you simply need to become aware of them. When you come to recognise this, you will recognise what a crucial role you play in your own recovery. Now, I share this information to empower you, not to suggest that you are in any way to blame for your illness. If you do, at any point, come to believe that you may have "made mistakes," know that there is no judgement from me, and please show compassion towards yourself and step away from any inner judgement that may arise within you. As you will see from my story, the wisdom I am sharing within *Finding the Energy to Thrive* has been hard-won. I have needed to make many mistakes and learn many lessons in order to recover my own health. So, I am not in a place of superiority: I very humbly share my learnings in order that you may take whatever resonates and helps you, and then adapt it to your own unique recovery journey.

Of all the chapters in the book, this one is least important in terms of providing information to support your recovery. So, you may choose not to read it. If you have read it, I invite you to use the following pages to answer some questions. There are no "right" or "wrong" answers to them. This is simply about helping you to uncover more awareness within yourself. You can write as much or as little as you desire. So, here are those questions:

What (if anything) do you recognise in my story that resonates with your own experience?

Have you had any lightbulb moments where something I have shared has given you a different perspective that feels helpful?

Is there anything in my story that you find challenging or unappealing? If so, name it and write down how/why it challenges you.

How are you feeling about accepting me as a guide through the CFS maze right now?

Notes

Notes

Chapter 2

Meet Your Driver

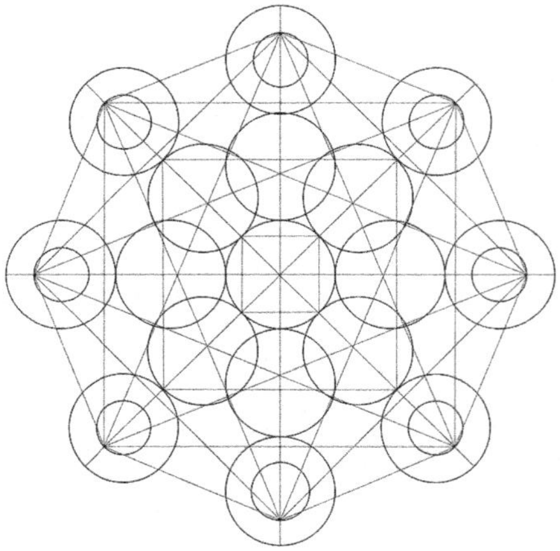

This chapter is designed to support you in becoming aware of your true Self. When you recognise and develop that portion of your inner world, you are able to rise above whatever is happening day to day. That allows you to find more peace and stability, which helps to keep your nervous system in its parasympathetic state. In that state, your body is receiving signals it is safe. That activates your natural biological healing mechanisms. It also allows you to access clarity of thought, creativity, compassion, and the capacity to connect more with your Self and with others. All those qualities will help you to navigate challenges with greater ease. It will help you to understand the messages your symptoms are trying to give you. It will also help you to evaluate potential treatment options and make wiser decisions about whether or not they could benefit you. The recovery journey is going to bring challenges, and the more you are able to access the peaceful state of witnessing, the less you will suffer as you travel this path. Developing this state is very much a practice. So, do not expect to change overnight, and do not judge or criticise yourself if you feel you are struggling to understand or practice any of this. You are just starting out on your journey, and I encourage you to take baby steps and be as compassionate towards yourself as you can. If you find this difficult, later chapters will reveal why that might be. So, just focus on doing your best and know you cannot get any of this "wrong."

The following bullet points outline the key themes in this chapter of the book:

- Whether or not you are aware of this, you have an internal dialogue constantly taking place inside your head. If you are aware of it, then that means you are also aware of the part of you that is listening to that dialogue. This part of you may be something you identify as your Soul, or as your True Self, or more simply as The Witness.

- That part has the capacity to step outside of your inner dialogue and simply observe it without engaging in the physical pains, uncomfortable emotions, or challenging thoughts that you are also experiencing. The part that engages in the physical, emotional, and mental aspects is your ego mind.

- If you wish to drive the optimal route through your personal maze, you will need to hand the car keys over to your True Self, not your ego self. There is every chance you have been driving with your ego self in charge up until this point. Most of us do, because we don't recognise there is another option. However, the ego self is not well placed to make the best decisions on our behalf. So, it is time to start getting acquainted with your True Self.

- We all have a natural tendency to judge everything we experience in life. We judge it to be "good" or "bad."

- In truth, this is not objective. The experience can be both "good" and "bad," depending on your perception, expectations, and desires. It can also be neither of those things. You are the one who chooses to judge what it is. Most of us do this subconsciously—reacting from the ego mind.

- So, how are you currently viewing your experience of CFS? Do you judge it to be "good" or "bad" or a mixture of both? Have you ever thought about it in those terms?

- Judgements do serve a useful purpose. Being able to understand that something was "bad" for us will keep us safe and prevent us from making the same mistake twice. Similarly, understanding that something is "good" for us can inspire us to bring more of it into our lives.

- However, when the ego-self is making the judgment, it is building upon its knowledge. These are basically the things it has been taught by others and the things it has observed from its own past experience. If that knowledge is true and wise, then helpful decisions may result from the process of judgement. This would be more like "discernment." But if the knowledge is somehow faulty, or applied in the wrong way, or to the wrong situation, then the judgement will be less helpful and any action guided by that judgement will also be sub-optimal.

- This principle applies to the way in which you have been—and will—approach your recovery from CFS. You may believe there are no reliable treatments available at present, so you are stuck. You may find a sense of peace and acceptance with this. Or, you may feel that living with CFS is so bad that you simply have to find a way out, and you will try whatever it takes. Once we remove judgement, we see both options are equally valid; they are simply choices to be made by each individual, depending on how they view their circumstances and the world around them.

- How can letting go of judgement support your recovery process? I am going to define judgement as the process of relying upon "knowledge" that may be influenced by prejudice: in other words, a belief system. The prejudice distorts our understanding of the true value of a treatment, so this may guide us to try something that is not supportive or to avoid something that could be really helpful.

- Ideally, we want to find a way to step outside of that. By identifying which beliefs (either yours or other people's) may be prejudiced in some way, we can step outside of them, take account of the prejudice, and try to weigh things up with discernment. Again, this is easier to achieve from the perspective of The Witness than from the perspective of the ego mind.

- The steps you take along your recovery path are always going to involve an element of uncertainty. Will they benefit you or not? Nobody can say for certain until you try it for yourself. The outcome of those experiments is going to bring about opportunities for judgement. You may be judging yourself, or you may find other people judging your decisions in wanting to try certain things and judging the outcome as they perceive it.

- The first thing you can do is to let go of other people's judgements. Recognise they are simply someone else's story.

They do not belong to you, and they need not harm you unless you choose to receive harm from them.

- The second thing you can do is become aware of your own judgement as it sits in the form of expectation. Every step you take on the recovery path is simply a step. It may bring immediate, obvious benefits. Or, it may seem to do nothing. It is also possible it feels like a step backwards. You are going to be tempted to judge all of these things and create stories about them. That is simply a waste of your precious energy.
- Start becoming aware of the internal dialogue that takes place whenever you try a new treatment or experience a new symptom. Are you internally criticising yourself? Are you using a lot of "absolutes" in your language (words like always, never, everyone, nobody)? These are simply creating a stress response in your body, which is not supportive of healing.
- Make a list of all the questions you have right now concerning your illness or available treatments.
- We are going to explore the stress response and how it contributes to remaining stuck in CFS in later chapters. For now, simply start to notice your language and try to reframe it. Rather than telling yourself an elaborate story that brings in judgements and criticism, try stepping back and sticking to the facts. The more you can develop the witness state and be with your emotions, but not drown in them, the more you will create an internal environment that supports recovery.

An invitation to practice

This part of your journey has all been about starting to develop self-awareness. So, in the interests of doing that, I have put together a few questions that will help to give you a clear picture of where you are right now. Self-awareness isn't only about having all the answers; it is also perfectly fine to observe that "you don't know" or to notice you are resisting this practice. That is all information, and it will all be helpful as we proceed. With that in mind, I invite you to start answering the following questions:

What symptoms are you experiencing at the moment?

Are there any symptoms you have previously experienced which are not causing you problems right now?

What treatments have you tried in the past?

Did they help you, and in what way?

Which of the following emotions do you feel now, or do you recognise feeling at some point in the past? (Please tick all that apply and write down anything else you can think of.)

- □ Anger at yourself
- □ Anger at doctors/the medical profession
- □ Anger at friends/family
- □ Powerlessness
- □ Lack of hope
- □ Fear
- □ Confusion
- □ Bitterness
- □ Shame
- □ Guilt
- □ Numbness/emptiness
- □ Worthlessness
- □ Self-hatred
- □ Joyfulness
- □ Hopefulness
- □ Compassion for yourself
- □ Love for yourself
- □ Empowerment

As you have been following this journaling exercise, have you noticed any judgement coming up?

Have you been judging your symptoms/treatments or making up stories about what they mean?

Do you notice any judgement of yourself as you consider what emotions you're feeling?

You may find it strange I am asking you to list all these things that you already know. But there is value in writing it down so that you become clear about your experience. This is all about developing clarity and self-awareness, which are critical if you want to take the shortest possible route to finding your energy again.

Now that you have recorded your answers, I would like you to put this journal away for today. Tomorrow, please take it out and re-read your words as an observer reading the words of somebody else. What do you notice? Are your thoughts more positive or negative? Are you criticising yourself at all? Do you use words like "never," or "always," or "everyone," or "nobody"? Those words are absolutes that often indicate we are feeling stuck and powerless. There is nothing wrong with you if you do notice any of these things about your writing and perception of yourself and CFS. They are perfectly normal responses to the situation in which you find yourself. I simply invite you to begin noticing this, and to begin exploring whether you are able to create some balance. For example, if you wrote something like "none of the treatments work for me," are you able to reframe it to something more like "I haven't found anything that works for me yet, and I will keep deepening my understanding and seeking new options," or to "I haven't found anything to help me. I accept that I feel [insert how you feel], and I am just going to be kind and loving towards myself today"?

Notes

Notes

Chapter 3

Meet Your Vehicle

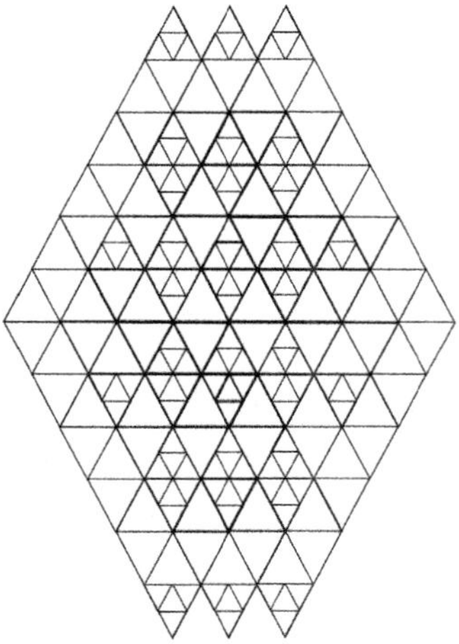

This chapter explores the idea that the way we view health, disease, and our bodies has a huge impact on our beliefs about the causes of illness and the best treatments for it. So, if you place CFS within the model used by conventional Western medicine, the illness makes no sense and has no effective treatment or cure. When you place CFS within a different model, one which sees the body as being interconnected with the mind, the spirit, and the wider environment, the illness suddenly makes a lot more sense and pathways to recovery begin to open up. If you have been approaching your recovery from a particular belief system, you may have been overlooking avenues that could help you. It is simple to become aware of the beliefs you hold and to decide which you desire to keep and which you are willing to change. Then, begin exploring from the perspective of a new belief system, and you are likely to discover new paths that could lead to exciting new places. The journaling prompts at the end of this chapter are inviting you to recognise your current beliefs and to examine them. I am not forcing you to change anything; simply to become aware of your model of health, disease, and your body. You may decide you wish to adapt your model today. Or, maybe you change nothing right now, but evolution will take place later on. Then again, perhaps you are completely satisfied that your understanding is absolutely correct, and you will never wish to change anything. Remember, build upon the Witness state so that you can see yourself with compassion and without judgement, and just remain curious as to what might unfold for you.

The following bullet points summarise the ideas discussed in chapter 3:

- Conventional Western medicine is (mostly) built upon the idea that a disease/illness is caused by a pathogen ("Germ") attacking the body.
- In that model, the solution to curing disease is to simply identify and eradicate the pathogen.
- Research has been unable to identify a single pathogen—or even a common set of pathogens – that cause CFS, so the illness seems to be a mystery, and that may be why, in the past, it has been viewed as something that could simply be hypochondria. This is also why you are likely to be told there is no reliable treatment or cure for your condition at the moment.
- An alternative view of disease, "Terrain Theory," places more emphasis on the basic health of the body—the "Terrain."
- This view suggests that if the body is basically healthy (functioning optimally), then it will be able to fight off a pathogen or other attack. That explains why two people can be

exposed to the same pathogen, and one may become ill while the other remains unaffected.

- Disease occurs when the body is not functioning optimally, so it is not equipped to fight off attacks. Rather than focusing on "killing attackers," we should be focusing on increasing the basic health of the body (Terrain).
- This model also allows us to understand that disease doesn't always have to be rooted in a pathogen. Lifestyle also has an important role to play.
- In this model, recovery from CFS can be accomplished by understanding—and correcting—all the areas of basic health, including things like optimal diet, cleaning out toxins, and so on. Functional Medicine follows this approach to support and create recovery.
- Instead of trying to explain CFS in one or another model, it may be more helpful to explore it as a combination of both.
- So, there may be a single pathogen or a set of pathogens that attacked the body at one time. Either they have not been effectively eradicated (killed/removed), or the body is still being exposed to them at the same time it is trying to get rid of them.
- We need to take a broader view of what we mean by Pathogen. This can include viruses, bacteria, infections, toxic chemicals, and emotions. All of these things signal to the body's cells that they are in danger.
- It is not enough to simply remove the Pathogen. The cells will also have sustained long-term damage from the attack. The body's natural healing system is equipped to deal with that. But the healing process requires energy, resources, and a

supportive environment to carry out this work. So, all of these factors need to be in place to complete the recovery process.

- In the Western world (commonly, at least), we have been taught to view ourselves as separate parts: a body, mind, emotions, and (maybe) a spirit/soul.
- This can lead to the view that any symptoms experienced in the physical body must have their roots and need healing in the physical body. Symptoms experienced in the mind have their roots and require healing in the mind, and so on.
- This immediately restricts where we look for answers when we are facing health issues. So, we can end up missing critical paths to recovery.
- What if we looked at those separate parts as elements of a single whole with a complex inter-relationship?
- Some of those elements fall in the physical realm (things we can see, hear, touch, smell, taste). Others fall into the "Energetic" realm—a state governed by frequency or "sense."
- Viewed through this lens, symptoms occurring in one part of the body may have their root cause in another part. So, simply addressing the symptom without addressing the root cause prevents the body from completing the healing cycle.
- This model accepts the complexities of CFS, but it also opens doors to exploring areas we might overlook but which may be key to recovery.

An Invitation to Practice

I would like you to reflect on how you feel about this chapter by answering the following questions:

What do you *think* about the models we've been exploring in this chapter?

Have you come across any of these ideas before?

How much of this makes logical sense to you?

Or does it all feel confusing: maybe you don't understand the point of this?

And if you don't know what to think right now, that's OK too—just note that down.

How do you *feel* about the material in this chapter?

Is it bringing up a feeling of hope that this might be a new path you haven't previously considered?

Perhaps you are feeling scared that I'm about to take you down paths you don't wish to explore?

Or is this making you feel angry or resentful, feeling that I am spouting some kind of rubbish here?

Are you feeling any shame or guilt or self-blame?

Is this starting to make lightbulbs switch on?

Or something else entirely?

And even if you don't know how you feel, that's your answer, and it's a perfectly good answer.

Lastly, building on the last practice: are you noticing any judgement coming up as you consider all this?

Are you judging yourself?

Are you judging me?

You can write at length if you really want to explore how you think and feel about these ideas. Or, if your energy is low, it's fine to keep your answers short. There are no "right" or "wrong" answers here. And, believe it or not, just noticing that you don't even know the answer is also very valuable information. I am asking you to do this so that you can become more aware of what you think and feel about your experience of CFS.

Notes

Notes

Chapter 4

Your Bioenergetic Body

This chapter introduces a very different model for understanding your body. This is the biofield, or energy body. You may recognise the concept if you have ever heard people talking about your aura. Yet, most people in the Western world assume this is some sort of spurious thing that is really rather woo-woo. I believe that is because the aura is most often spoken of in spiritual circles. Our Western belief system tends to focus intently on the material world and suggest that a spiritual world doesn't really exist. Or, at best, that it is an optional thing we may like to believe and explore to find some comfort. In reality, the spiritual world is every bit as real as the material world. In fact, when you take it outside any discussion related to spirituality, you discover it is a concept built upon physics; specifically, quantum physics. So, it is both spiritual—metaphysical—and scientific. So, far from being an "alternative" model we can take up or discard according to our belief system, the Energy Field is a fundamental part of our Universe. It underpins the material world. Your biofield is not simply an "alternative" way of examining your body; it is the foundation of your body. Whatever is manifesting in your physical body and physical reality is rooted in the Energy body or biofield. Imagine if you believed that your garden only existed in the layer you can see—the layer above ground level. With this worldview, it would be natural to try to remove an unwanted plant by simply cutting its stem at soil level. However, the plant would grow a new stem, branches, leaves, and flowers. Only when you recognise a critical portion of the plant exists below the visible portion of your garden—in the soil underneath the surface—can you make a more permanent change. If you dig down and remove the entire root, then the plant will not re-grow.

Now, on some level, we have this awareness within the physical body. We are seeking the "root cause" of an illness. The current research in CFS has been unsuccessful in discovering that. My personal experience has led me to understand this is because we have only been looking above the surface. Very few people in the medical profession, at present, are willing to acknowledge the presence of the biofield. Those who have acknowledged it are only just beginning to explore and understand it. Yet, we have more understanding than we know if we are prepared to widen our perspective and apply some—not all—ideas of metaphysics to what we know from quantum physics regarding energy fields. My personal journey through this realm is what ended up taking me from a place where I was "managing" my CFS to a place of genuine recovery. You may or may not need to take the same journey, but if you have already thoroughly explored all other avenues, I would recommend turning your attention to this area to see what new paths it opens for you.

The following bullet points summarise the main information shared in this chapter:

- Your body is a complex system of communication. The basic mechanics of biology and chemistry only explain part of this story. To understand the full extent of the body's ability to communicate and thus regulate itself, we need to appreciate that it also encompasses an energy field.
- In 1992, the Office of Alternative Medicine in the USA agreed on a term to describe this energy field—the biofield—and researchers began to study it in order to appreciate how it works and how we can use energy medicine to enhance healing.
- Your biofield is best understood as a wireless communication system. It communicates via frequency and resonance. The biofield contains the blueprint for perfect health, but distortions in the Information in the field, or blockages in communication, can end up giving your cells incorrect messages. This results in disease.
- Traditional cultures have always understood a concept of the biofield. It may be called by different names: aura, prana, chi, but the principle is the same. If you wish to create health, you need to ensure that the energy in this field is free to flow and communicate with accuracy.
- The biofield communicates using waveform and frequency. Disturbances in the waveforms will result in miscommunication, which, in turn, causes your physical cells and systems to begin acting in ways that result in the symptoms we label as disease.
- Think of this like your mobile/cell phone: if you pass through a spot with a weak signal, you may lose the call or at least find

it becomes distorted. The same can happen in the biofield's communication system.

- Your biofield is communicating internally and also with the environment around it. So, everything in our environment has its own unique biofield. Your body can recognise the frequency of other natural biofields and interpret their information to know how to use resources like food, water, and light to support energy production.
- External factors like toxins, viruses, and bacteria and toxic thoughts and emotions can cause disruptions in the biofield. If your field is able to recognise and react to these, you will remain healthy and in balance. When the biofield doesn't have the capacity to respond, it will adapt to the challenge, allowing you to survive but possibly not to thrive.
- Understanding the biofield and how it works gives us a model for making sense of CFS.
- It can explain the complexity of symptoms: in the field, everything is interrelated, so a change in one area will cause change across the entire field.
- It can also explain the difference in how the illness begins and the shape it takes from one individual to another.
- Most importantly, this model offers a powerful way to generate recovery.
- Discovering Energy medicine and working with my biofield proved to be the final piece of the puzzle in my own recovery.
- Prior to that, I had been working from the perspective of trying to understand linear systems. In a sense, the mechanics of how my body was working—or not! The deeper we delve

into those mechanics, the more complex it becomes, and the more we end up hitting brick walls or circular "chicken and egg" situations.

- Stepping back and understanding the biofield as a whole field of communication and governance allows us to step out of that complexity, focus on identifying and correcting the distorted Information in the field, and allow it to flow down into the physical body and create healing.
- So, our next port of call will be to discover what Information is carried in the field and how we can begin to analyse and understand it.

Your invitation to practice:

I invite you to pause and explore how you think and feel about this chapter. Please use the following questions as writing prompts. As always, you can write as much or as little as you wish. Remember to take note of the things towards which you feel judgemental. And remember that "I don't know" is always an acceptable answer.

Are you open to the idea that you have a biofield and it has an impact on your physical body?

If you said "yes," does this idea change anything about how you view your illness?

If you said "no," why do you feel or think this way?

Looking back to the time before you became ill, can you identify things in your environment and lifestyle that might have caused disruption in your field or not been supportive of your physical body? Think about the following:

- What was your diet like?
- How much sleep did you get?
- How much did you exercise?
- Were you exposed to a lot of chemical toxins?
- How was your immune system—did you often get ill?
- How did you feel emotionally?
- How were your stress levels?
- What were your relationships with other people like?
- Are you aware of any traumatic events in your past or present?
- Can you think of any other possible contributing factors?

Notes

Chapter 5

The Four Levels of Creation

This chapter introduces you to the model I call *Four Levels of Creation*. It also explores the first layer in this model. The reason for sharing this material is to help you appreciate that you do not exist in isolation. Although you most likely feel like a separate, disconnected entity, you are deeply connected to the entire Universe and everything within it. Why does that matter? Well, when you are in connection with any element, you are both affecting it, and it is affecting you. So, in the case of CFS, there are aspects outside of what you consider to be "you" that are impacting you and may turn out to be root causes of your illness. So, if you are trying to recover, you need to be aware of these aspects and address any that are impacting you.

I wish to acknowledge that these ideas may feel challenging for you. If that is the case, I invite you to try to maintain an open mind and simply remain curious. I am not asking you to immediately believe or subscribe to everything here. Simply become aware of these ideas. In future, they may become relevant to you. When that happens, you can revisit this material and explore it more deeply. If you are ready for that deeper exploration right now, then these ideas have the power to unlock profound transformation for you.

The following bullet points summarise the information shared in chapter 5 of the book:

- We are now going to build on the idea that our "body" is one thing, including its physical, mental, emotional, and spiritual elements. The physical body can be sensed with our five basic senses: it is matter and makes up the physical body element of the human. The other elements are not directly sensed by our basic senses, so they may appear invisible or intangible: they are energy and make up the energy body element of the human.

- Symptoms occurring at one level may have their root cause at that level as well—or the root cause and symptom may be located on different levels.

- If you are seeking "healing" rather than "symptom management," it is vital to understand the four levels so you can identify where the root cause sits and address it at that level.

- As we move on to explore the different levels, some of the language and ideas I share may seem to belong in a spiritual context. But I am not meaning them to be viewed as "religious" or "New Age." They may share common ground with those movements, but they are also independent, and it is possible to work with the Four Levels of Creation model to effect recovery independently of your existing beliefs and without needing to reject or change those beliefs if you do not wish it.

- Different models of Creation have existed for as long as humanity has existed. Ayurvedic Medicine, Traditional Chinese Medicine, Integrative Healers, and now German New Medicine all use this type of model. Yet, it is not—currently—taught in conventional medical school.

- We take a brief look at the five-level model used by Dr Dietrich Klinghardt to heal chronic disease. This has helped many patients with CFS.

- The reason I work with the Four Levels model is because it is the model that I used on my recovery path and the model that I now apply in my own practice to help others find recovery.

- The creative process travels through four layers, starting with an idea: pure energy—a particle. We can think of this at the top of a pyramid: the Universe—Unity Consciousness. The creative process forms that idea into a "thing": matter. In this case, your physical body sitting at the bottom of the pyramid.

- The intervening two layers—Intuitive, then Psycho-Emotional—guide the creative process. You might think of this like a blueprint, guiding the energy particles via Information to take on wave-form, which ultimately compresses into matter, loosely following a path where particles become atoms, then cells, then organs/systems, and then a complete human body.

- In metaphysical terms, Unity Consciousness is the basic idea that we are all one: a single creative force with multiple individual expressions.

- Our physical awareness has become rooted in individual experience; most of us have forgotten that we are all one. Those who "awaken" may suddenly remember this idea of being one with the Universe and begin to seek Enlightenment. They are seeking to access this experience of Oneness—we call it Samadhi.
- The work of scientist Dr Robert Lanza supports this idea. His model Biocentrism demonstrates we are not dropped into a pre-existing, independent Universe. We are active creators, creating our lived experience all the time. So, we are the Universe, and we are also experiencing the Universe. We are not separate from the creative Source.
- In individual human experience, the creative step that takes place at this level is the idea. An idea pops into your head out of nowhere.
- In scientific terms, the creative step at this level is the particle(s) appearing in a vacuum, ready to combine with other particles and begin to form atoms.
- In order to begin to think about how this level affects your recovery, you need to understand the principles of how it operates. In scientific terms, this is a Field. A field contains individual particles and Information. There is a two-way interaction between the individual and the field, governed by the Information. So, the Information shapes how the particles interact, and the interactions of the particles feed back to reshape the Information, which then reshapes the particle interactions further.
- In terms of humanity, this interaction between the individual and the collective can take place at the physical level—physical

interaction with a group—and at the energetic level—mental/ emotional interaction with others.

- From a religious perspective, we would be re-framing this idea to talk in terms of prayer and outcomes as the channel of communication between the individual and the Creator Being—Divinity. Yet, that can often involve a perception of separation: the human is separate from the Divine.
- Bringing this away from religion and into a more metaphysical realm, we see the human as an individuated part of the Unity Consciousness—the particle as an individuated part of the Field—and in that model when we offer up a "prayer," we aren't talking to "other." We are connecting to the part of ourselves that sits at the level of Unity Consciousness.
- In this model, "prayer" is a very specific term for a more general concept. Every desire, idea, and thought can be a "prayer." So, the question becomes, are we creating consciously or unconsciously? The answer: both. Therefore, your experience will reflect both aspects. This means changing your experience can be a matter of uncovering where you are creating unconsciously—unaware of—thought and behaviour patterns, and changing those. This is what we will explore in full in part three, as we unravel what Trauma is and how it impacts the conscious mind, subconscious mind, and physical body.
- This model implies, in order for healing to take place at the Unity Consciousness level, you need to consciously partner with the Creative Source. Religion offers us a way to do this through the power of prayer or faith healing. Anecdotally, this may work.
- Scientific study and analysis of healing through prayer has proven inconclusive. Why is that? Possibly the design of the

studies has been poor. Possibly we are seeking to use a tool—science—to study a subject inherently based on faith which cannot be proved or disproved.

- The model with which I work sees individuals as remaining connected to the Creative Source. Individuals exist because the Creative Source wished to know itself and chose to do this by individuating so that it could experience infinite possibilities. In order to know anything, you need to know what that thing IS and what it IS NOT. This means the individuated part must have the freedom to create "good" and "bad" —the polarities. In order for that to work effectively, the individuated part must have free will so it is not being orchestrated by its Creative Source—it is free to explore and create whatever it dreams up, and the Creative Source will experience those dreams and gain greater awareness of itself.
- If the individual is free to create consciously and subconsciously, then in order for the desired outcome to be realized, both conscious and subconscious minds must be seeking the same goal. If they are not, the Creative Source cannot override the free will of either part. The individual must recognise the conflict and request assistance in making a change. Until then, there may be a disparity between the individual's conscious desire and the physical reality. It may appear that this is a case of a prayer not being answered. In reality, it reflects an unresolved conflict between the individual's conscious and subconscious desires.
- This will become more pertinent and apparent in section three when we explore Trauma and its relationship to CFS.
- It is important to understand that the Creative process is not a one-off, linear process. It is cyclical and continuous. In

other words, the process may feed down from idea to physical reality, but it doesn't stop there. The physical reality then feeds back up to the Creative Source, allowing that source to make alterations which feed down to allow the physical expression to expand and evolve. For example, your physical body is constantly regenerating itself as older cells die off and are replaced by newer cells.

- Second, we are examining this in a linear fashion in order to help make the model easier to grasp. But in fact, all the levels are operating together all at once, not one at a time one after the other.

- The levels are not equal in terms of the impact they have on our experience. Only 1% of our physical experience has its origins at the physical level, 19% of our physical experience originates from the psycho-emotional level, and 80% of that physical experience originates from the Intuitive level. So, if you are seeking to create lasting change, focusing only on the physical level is going to bring about limited results. Focusing on the Intuitive level will have a much greater impact, and changes made at that level will automatically feed down to express at the physical level. However, complete healing needs to address the issues at ALL levels.

An Invitation to Practice

I invite you to use the following questions to start noticing—and writing about—your reactions to this chapter.

How do you *feel* about it?

- Confused?

- Hopeful?

- Angry?

- Unsure how to answer that?

- Something else?

What do you *think* about the information in this chapter?

Does it sound similar to information you have heard before, or is it completely new to you?

Are you open to working with this model, or do you still feel that your body is a physical entity and nothing more?

Remember, there are no "wrong" answers here. Just note down whatever you feel, think, and notice. And if you are judging yourself—or me—make a note of that as well. This is just information-gathering at this stage.

Notes

Notes

Chapter 6

Sacred Geometry – The Intuitive Level

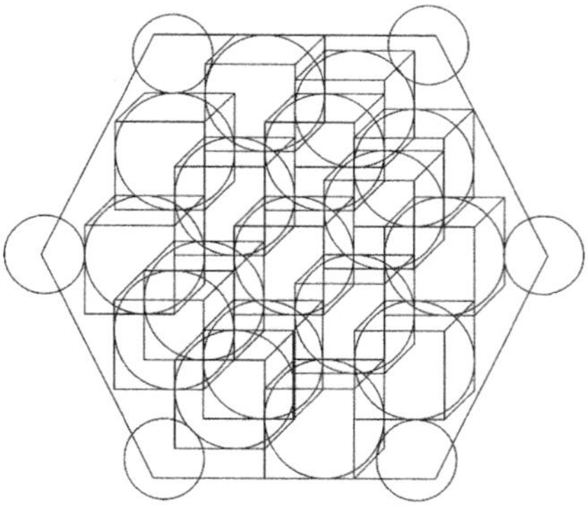

This chapter explores the next level, the Intuitive Level. Again, the information covered here may, at first glance, appear more related to spirituality rather than health. Depending on your existing belief system, some of the areas covered here may feel challenging to explore. Once again, I remind you to simply remain curious and open. If you are reading things that conflict with your existing worldview, I am not trying to say your current view is wrong. In many areas, this is simply a new perspective you may not have considered before. It doesn't necessarily need to replace your existing ideas, but it can be integrated to create an expanded awareness within you.

Some of the information in this chapter will make more sense after you have understood more about your nervous system and its role in keeping you stuck in the chronic fatigue loop. We cover that in part three of Finding the Energy to Thrive. If you have already invested a lot of time and money in exploring treatment options and still have not found a sustainable recovery, then the information in this chapter may be key to giving you a new perspective on your illness. From this new perspective, you can explore new pathways, and one of those may turn out to be the one that supports your recovery. As with the last chapter, I wish to acknowledge that you may not be open to receiving this information right now. So, if that is the case, just know it is here to be explored in the future whenever you are ready to return to it.

The following bullet points summarise the information covered in chapter 6:

- This introduces the idea that, at this level, the building blocks are mathematics—specifically, geometry. Think of this as coded Information that determines the eventual shape of your physical creation.

- This is important because if you wish to make a change at any level, you need to use the tools that relate to its building blocks. So, in this case, we would need to change the Information—or coding—that is creating an outcome we find undesirable.

- If we examine this level from a spiritual or metaphysical perspective, then it is the level that contains the Akashic records. This is the record of all events coded into the fabric of the Universe. Note: this is mathematical/geometric coding that creates the record.

- We have a Universal Akash, and we also each have our own personal Akash—the record of everything our individuated soul has experienced during its existence across multiple lifetimes. That personal record is our Karma.

- This is not just a theoretical idea or metaphysical concept: brilliant scientists are putting forth theories and carrying out experiments that support the possibility of there being a coded Information store which creates the world we experience.

- In many cultures, past lives are an accepted fact. In the West, we may be a little more sceptical. Yet many people report having past life memories, and there is a fascinating body of psychiatric research into this area.

- This is an invitation to keep an open mind because some clues to your current life experience may be coming in from past lives.

- On slightly less controversial ground, we are also gathering evidence that the traumatic experiences of one generation can be inherited by later generations. So, if your grandparents lived through a traumatic event like World War II, that can have caused alterations in their gene expression, which are then passed on down to you, and which will have a direct impact on your own Central Nervous System.

- We tend to think of Karma as being about a system of punishment and reward. This implies a judgement by some external "other."

- In fact, Karma is really about a system of consequences. There is no judgement involved. The system of Karma allows the Universal Consciousness to experience its full potential through individuating. A choice made by the individuated Soul in one lifetime will impact the experiences of that Soul in the next lifetime so the Universal Consciousness, through the individuated Soul, can fully experience a concept from both the perspective of what it is and what it is not.

- Infinite individuated Souls, all creating infinite experiences, allow the Universal Consciousness to fully know itself—know all that is possible.
- We explore more nuances of Karma. In between lives, the individuated soul chooses what it wishes to experience to complete Karmic lessons. These choices may be made in conjunction with other souls who agree to help by creating circumstances that allow the desired experience to take place. But we have no memory of this between-life—or indeed, past-life—experience. So, we view our current physical existence as positive or negative.
- We also retain free will. So, if we have chosen to experience something that would allow us to complete a Karmic debt and grow, we have the free will to decide how we respond to that event. Do we view it as an opportunity for growth and healing? Or do we see it as an unjust challenge and perhaps even accrue more Karmic debt from responding unwisely to it?
- You might want to view this as a "nice little idea" or as completely crazy, or you might want to consider that this model of existence could have huge implications for the story you are telling yourself about your health challenges.
- In more practical terms, we can view this level of creation as a step in a project to build a house. This step involves the mathematical calculations of room size, load bearing, etc., which will determine how successfully you build your house.
- Viewed through the lens of physics at the previous level, we introduced particles into a vacuum. They are currently moving around chaotically, without structure, until at this level we introduce the Information—the blueprint that tells them what physical form to take.

- From an epigenetic perspective, the blueprint encoded in your DNA can change its expression by altering the information it receives from its environment. So, your health may not be set in stone.
- The purpose of exploring this level is to understand how it can be impacting your physical experience and what you can do to make alterations if you need to.
- If you felt your symptoms were rooted at this level, the swiftest, most effective way to change those root causes is by changing the Information coded into your biofield. Imprinted meditations and NES Infoceuticals are both designed to do this.

An Invitation to Practice

This chapter has covered a lot of ground and is likely to elicit a lot of different responses in you. So, I invite you to explore how you feel by answering the following questions:

Which parts of this chapter felt good or brought up positive emotions in you?

Which parts of this chapter felt challenging or brought up negative emotions in you?

What do you *think* about the material in this chapter?

Have you ever had any experiences that you feel might be related to reincarnation or past lives? If yes, name them.

Do you have any fears that seem a little irrational, and you can't track back to events of which you are aware in this lifetime? If yes, name them.

Think about the experiences of your ancestors and the community in which you grew up and in which you now live. Which of those experiences might have been traumatic? This could be examples like mine—grandparents living through a war. It could be cultural or historic—racism or sexism. It could be current in the community in which you were raised or live now—poverty, racism, sexism, etc. Make a few notes about these experiences.

Notes

Chapter 7

The Psycho-Emotional Level

This chapter explores the psycho-emotional level and the concepts found within that layer of the model. You may have come across people talking about the mind-body connection. Perhaps these people have suggested that some—or all—of your illness is being generated through this connection. I know when someone first suggested that idea to me, I did not receive it well. I felt as though I was being accused of making the illness up, of being a hypochondriac, and that my entire experience was being invalidated. So, I wish to emphasise that CFS is a very physical illness. You will experience it in your physical body, and it will impact your physical world. Yet, as we delve deeper into the idea that we are more than just a physical entity, this idea of a mind-body connection begins to make more sense. In this chapter, I will also be exploring areas that are not often spoken of in the context of the mind-body model. Understanding more about this should help you see that you are not to blame. You did not consciously create your CFS, and you are not consciously remaining ill. So, again, at first glance, the areas we explore may feel challenging to your existing beliefs. If you are not yet ready to embrace them, that is OK. The most important thing is to simply become aware of other ideas. Perhaps you will feel able to integrate them into your existing worldview, or perhaps they are something you wish to set aside for now. Either is fine: trust that you will find whatever you need at the optimal time for you. If you are early in your recovery journey, then your answers may lie at the physical level. However, if you have already explored many options at that level and found no answers, this information invites you to recognise this is not the end of the road. There are more layers to explore whenever you feel ready.

The following bullet points share the main ideas explored in chapter 7:

- The psycho-emotional level creates 19% of your physical experience. That doesn't mean your physical symptoms aren't real: simply that their root cause is in thoughts, emotions, and beliefs. So, if you want to experience improvement in your physical symptoms, you need to heal the disruptive emotions/thoughts/beliefs.

- These thoughts/emotions/beliefs reside in the biofield as waves with a frequency. Waves of a particular frequency will attract waves of a similar frequency.

- If you detect problems caused by low-frequency waves, you can raise their frequency by exposing them to higher-frequency waves and allow the two sets to synchronise at the higher level.

- These principles of Quantum Physics underline how we can create change at this level and experience consequent improvements in energy and health.

- This level also has metaphysical implications. In the last chapter, we looked at Karma. That is stored as coding in the Intuitive level, but it also has an emotional charge stored at this Psycho-Emotional level.

- If you have incarnated with a lot of Karma to clear, you may be carrying a lot of low-frequency vibrational energy in your biofield. This will attract low-frequency events or challenges. They are not designed to be a punishment but rather an invitation to see the low-frequency patterns and take steps to raise their frequency.

- Thoughts, emotions, and beliefs are held as Energy vibrating at a particular frequency in your biofield. These end up manifesting as behavioural patterns and physical symptoms that feel challenging.

- If you wish to adjust or improve symptoms resulting from low-frequency thoughts/emotions/beliefs, you need to use treatments that work on the level of frequency.

- You may not have considered this before, but your illness might be here as an invitation to experience growth. How do you achieve this? By becoming curious and examining your symptoms, learning lessons, and stopping your resistance to them. You have greater healing power than you may realise.

Your Invitation to Practice

Please record your responses and reflections in answer to the following questions:

Has this chapter brought up any uncomfortable emotions for you? If so, which emotions, and which parts of the chapter brought them up?

What do you think about the ideas in this chapter?

Make a list of all the things that you wish to be able to do in life, but which you can't do because of your CFS.

Make a list of all the ways in which having CFS has improved your life. For example, maybe you feel happier spending time on your own, or happier because you don't have to do a job you dislike, or maybe someone looks after you. To be clear, this is NOT me suggesting that you are deliberately making up your illness or even that you are enjoying the experience. I am sure neither of those things is true. But every experience in life brings us challenges and benefits, and I am inviting you to view your CFS experience from two perspectives. Believe it or not, this understanding is going to help you see where you can focus most effectively on your recovery path. So, even though this request is going to challenge you, don't skip it!

Notes

Chapter 8

The Physical Level

This chapter is designed to bring everything together from the *Four Levels of Creation* model. So, we will be exploring how the previous levels feed into creating your experience at the physical level. Most of your awareness sits at this level, and this level will be your first point of exploration as you seek recovery from CFS. If you have already explored it comprehensively and still not found your elusive recovery path, then it may be time to explore the other levels. The information shared in this chapter is intended to help you understand how your physical experience is really the tip of the iceberg when it comes to understanding you and your illness. Although you may have been exploring very new territory, my intention is to bring you hope. Rather than believing there are no answers, and you are simply stuck in a state of misery, I hope this model has opened your eyes to new possibilities for exploration. These new avenues are ready whenever you feel a call to explore them. That may be today, or it may be some time in the future. It is also perfectly natural to still feel a lot of confusion about the relevance of any of this to your illness. If that is what you are experiencing right now, then the next section of *Finding the Energy to Thrive* should help you. It will start by exploring your physical symptoms and helping you to understand how and why they are manifesting. So, please take whatever resonates from this chapter for now: you may wish to return and explore it more deeply later on.

The following bullet points outline the main areas of exploration in chapter 8:

- The Physical level is where you are probably most familiar. This is where your physical body resides, along with everything else that you can see, hear, touch, taste, and smell. At this level, classical physics, biology, and chemistry govern things. In terms of disease and healing, the focus is primarily on biology and chemistry.

- Bringing all the levels together, you can use the analogy of building a house. At this level, the actual house appears. But whether it is complete and built as planned will be determined by how well the architect carried out the calculations, how accurately the draftsman drew the plans, and whether or not the builder followed the blueprint. If something is "wrong" with the house, you need to identify at which level of creation the original error occurred and to make the correction at that level. This makes perfect sense within the analogy of building a house, but have you ever considered what that means if you are building a body? The Four Levels of Creation model is about considering we may need to take a wider view of our physical symptoms and their origin if we wish to truly resolve them and heal.

- In each of the previous Levels of Creation, we have seen how each layer bleeds into the next: the issues at one layer have an impact on what happens in the next layer. The same is true with the physical level.
- We look at three discrete areas in which scientific research has shown a clear correlation between thoughts and feelings and the physical symptoms that result. In other words, the psycho-emotional level has a direct impact on the physical level. These three examples are: the science of Psychoneuroimmunology, our understanding of genetics, and the curious case of the symptomology of Multiple Personality Disorder.
- If you wish to focus purely on physiological symptoms and physical tools, then you may be looking at things like pharmaceutical drugs, surgery, nutritional supplements, and yoga—basically, a diverse range of different protocols that all work on the physiology, biology, or chemistry of the body in some way.
- If you are looking at some newer modalities, like PEMF therapy, EFT, and Vagus Nerve Stimulators, consider how they work. Are they focusing on biology and chemistry or are they using the principles of physics?
- At the end of the day, the important point is to recognise that we operate as a whole person and we need to be considering both the origin of problems and the tools to solve them from the perspective of all levels of our being.
- I briefly put the Four Levels of Creation model into my own recovery journey and explain why I feel that my personal

experience is testimony to the effectiveness of using this model for recovery.

- This sets up the next section of the book, where we will move back to looking at the physical experience of living with CFS and how that could map onto the model.

An Invitation to Practice

Once more, I invite you to use the following prompts to continue adding to your self-awareness.

How does this chapter make you feel?

Note down any emotions that you are feeling in response to this information. And if it doesn't make you feel anything, that's OK too—just make a note of that.

What do you think about the information in this chapter?

Note which ideas are new to you and which are familiar.

Has any of the information in this chapter changed the way you think and feel about the other levels of creation?

Bringing your focus back to your own experience, make a list of the symptoms you are currently experiencing. Considering each of your individual symptoms, or the set as a whole, answer the following questions:

Have you sought treatment for this symptom/symptom set?

Have you experienced any improvements as a result of any treatments?

Have any symptoms improved naturally? If so, what was happening at that time in your life?

Has any of the information in this section prompted you to think differently about where you are looking for answers about CFS?

Notes

Chapter 9

Exploring the Physical Symptoms of CFS

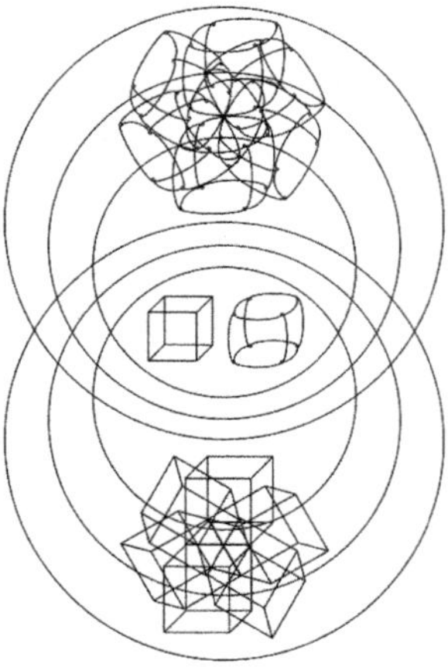

Contrary to popular belief, we have a pretty good understanding of *how* CFS manifests in the body. Although the illness has not received as much research or attention as other illnesses, it has been researched by some very brilliant minds. The results of that research have brought a good understanding of the various symptoms and many of the mechanisms through which they occur. The problem is that the research is still struggling to answer the question of *why*. My personal experience leads me to believe the reason we're missing that answer is because the focus is being directed into one area and ignoring the bigger picture. The entire purpose of *Finding the Energy to Thrive* has been to argue that we do have solutions and a much greater understanding than we realise. We simply need to join more dots and widen our search for answers. So, this chapter should help you to understand the basic mechanisms creating your CFS symptoms. There may even be something in the information that allows you to see your illness through a new lens and to try a new path which improves your experience. The ideas in this chapter are rather like the first set of breadcrumbs on a trail we will continue to follow through the next four chapters.

The following bullet points summarise the information shared in chapter 9:

- The range of different symptoms experienced by people living with CFS is huge. When listed, they appear to affect so many different systems within the body that it is hard to make sense of it all.

- Additionally, everyone's experience is subtly different: some people experience all the symptoms, others just a few. The severity also varies drastically from person to person. This all adds to the confusion.

- We have just explored the idea your body is greater than its physiology. It also has a biofield containing information about your mental and emotional state. I would like to suggest if we turn our focus to this idea and start looking at a root cause of stored trauma, everything about CFS begins to make much more sense.

- The 2016 ground-breaking research paper led by Dr. Robert Naviaux and Dr. Eric Gordon uncovered something called the Cell Danger Response. This is the idea that the body's cells have gone into an ongoing state of "hibernation" called dauer.

- This causes your cells to shut down and reduce the performance of tasks to an absolute minimum, in order to keep you safe from a threat and allow you to survive. Unfortunately, this state does not support "thriving."

- The perception you are under threat is coming from the Central Nervous System. The "threat" it is sensing is your stored trauma: physical, mental, and emotional.

- A lot of researchers have focused on their field of expertise—understandably—and this has led to argument and debate about which is "the one" thing that causes CFS.

- Taking a top-level perspective of all of those "causes," we can see they have a shared root. Each system viewed as being "responsible" for triggering or perpetuating CFS is actually controlled by the Central Nervous System.

- I invite you to turn things on their head. The Central Nervous System is sensing danger in its environment. It signals that danger to the cells, and they react according to a system designed to keep you safe and allow you to survive. Logically, then, your body has not "gone wrong." It is doing exactly what it has been programmed to do. The problem is not with your symptoms; it is with the environment triggering the danger signal.

- For me, letting go of the idea of trying to "get rid" of my symptoms and turning, instead, to working on ways of creating energy led to recovery.

- We need to change our environment at the physical, mental, and emotional levels, which means addressing issues that sit in all layers of the Four Levels of Creation model.

Your Invitation to Practice

Please use the following prompts to write about how this new information is making you think and feel. It's OK if you don't understand everything here: we still have a lot more ground to explore. So, you may want to come back to this chapter after we have taken a look at more of your maze.

Can you follow the logic of the argument I am trying to present?

If not, which part isn't making sense to you?

How is this information making you feel: what emotions are coming up as you read it?

Is this bringing up questions for you? If so, write them down.

Notes

Chapter 10

Meet Your Central Nervous System

The previous chapter connected the physical symptoms of CFS back to the central nervous system. In this chapter, we begin to explore that system. When you first learn about it, you may be tempted to feel as though you are being told that your illness is rooted in your mind, not your body. That may, in turn, lead you to feel a sense of shame, self-blame, or frustration. So, this chapter aims to give you a new understanding and a different perspective on the idea of the mind-body connection. This information will, ultimately, empower you to take control of your experience. The ideas I am sharing in here will be developed further in the next chapter, so please remember that I am inviting you to gradually build up a new picture of your experience. If there are things that do not immediately make sense, that's OK. You can revisit this information as often as you need.

The following bullet points summarise the information shared in chapter 10:

- Your Central Nervous System (CNS) is like the master controller of your body. The Autonomic Nervous System (ANS) is one of the oldest evolutionary parts of your brain, sometimes called the Reptilian part. Its sole purpose is to help you survive. So, it is constantly assessing your environment—external and internal—and communicating with your cells to let them know if they are safe or in danger.

- Modern life is complex: Emotional challenges are now more common than physical dangers, but your ANS has not adapted to understand that. So, a negative emotion can create as big a danger signal as coming face to face with a sabre-toothed tiger. The difference is that the emotion won't kill you, but the sabre-toothed tiger might. However, your ANS doesn't understand that.

- As our brains evolved, we developed the mammalian systems wired for social contact and able to understand more of the nuances of life. However, if the ANS has already kicked in and fired off the danger warning, our access to the more conscious, rational, decision-making parts of the brain is shut down.

- Your ANS has three possible states: rest/digest—parasympathetic or Ventral Vagal, fight/flight—sympathetic, and freeze—Dorsal Vagal.

- Ideally, you should be living in the parasympathetic state: in this mode, your body is maintaining its systems, you are open to social engagement, and all is well. This state promotes health and healing.

- If your ANS detects a threat, it will take you up into the fight-flight state, signalling all your cells to prepare to either fight off an attack or run away to safety. In this state, essential maintenance tasks are temporarily suspended to focus all your energy on saving your life. This is supposed to be a temporary state, requiring a lot of energy to sustain it.

- So, if your body gets stuck in that state for too long, it will run out of energy to sustain the fight-flight state. If your ANS does not feel the danger has passed, it has no choice but to move into freeze. This is a low-energy state, but NOT a state of safety. So, in this state, you will be shut down, dissociated, and still not maintaining your organs and systems.

- Your body will naturally try to move down from this state and back to parasympathetic mode. But, to get there, it has to pass back through the fight-flight. If the original danger is still felt to be present, it will not manage to exit the fight-flight, but end up running out of energy again and returning to freeze.

- This can become a permanent cycle, which we term a "maladaptive nervous system." In this cycle, your body is consistently struggling to maintain itself: this state does not promote health or healing.

- It is really helpful to understand the emotional links. If we have trouble processing specific emotions—for example, anger—they can trigger us to become stuck in the loop of fight-flight-freeze-fight-flight-freeze.

- We will elaborate on this idea in a later chapter, but it is important to remember that none of this is your fault.

- There is another layer to this model. We each have a different Window of Tolerance. This is my way of describing the "bandwidth" of your parasympathetic state.

- If you have a low bandwidth—narrow Window of Tolerance, then a small incident can trigger a full trauma response. If your bandwidth is wider, then you have a greater capacity to feel the stress but also maintain access to the rational, thinking part of your brain, which can regulate your ANS back down to safety.

- It is important to understand that stress and trauma are not about the event itself; they are a description of how your body reacts to the event.

- Your Central Nervous System develops in the womb and during your early life. It learns how to adapt to stressful events and re-regulate itself from the mother and primary caregiver. If your early years were spent in an unsupportive environment, this has a lasting impact on your nervous system, setting up patterns you will carry into adulthood.

- It will also be affected by ancestral trauma: gene expression can be changed by experiencing trauma, and altered gene expression can be inherited through multiple generations.

- The good news is you can repair your system and reprogram it so it returns to supporting your health and healing. Trauma is your body's reaction to an event, not the event itself. So, whilst it would not be possible to "undo" the event, it is possible to heal the reaction.

An Invitation to Practice

Once again, I would like you to reflect on how you are feeling and any new understanding emerging from this information. Please answer the following questions:

How do you *feel* about the information in this chapter?

What do you *think* about it?

Do you have any awareness of how your body changes state? For example, do you notice when you move into fight/flight, or live in freeze?

Do you feel your emotions in your body? Are you aware of them coming and going?

How much of the time are you aware of what your body is experiencing, and how much time do you spend in your head, thinking and analysing?

Please remember, there are no "right" or "wrong" answers to any of these questions. This is simply to build up information. So, if you do catch yourself judging your responses or wanting to judge your past life experiences, just notice this happening, make a note of what is coming up, and politely set those judgements to one side.

Notes

Chapter 11

What Is Trauma?

Even if you understand the critical role that your nervous system plays in regulating your body, you may still be a little confused about how the nervous system is triggered into a maladaptive state. Many people still confuse stress and trauma, not realising these are two subtly different things. We are told to avoid stress, yet a certain amount of the right kind of stress is necessary to help us grow and thrive. Very often it is trauma, rather than stress that needs resolving. Even when that distinction has been made correctly, there is still a great deal of misunderstanding about trauma. This lack of understanding can lead to recommendations for ineffective treatments or to an assumption that treatment just isn't possible at all. So, this is another crucial layer to understand if you have already explored many avenues in the hope of recovery and found yourself getting nowhere. It is very possible that you have been—accidentally—exploring the wrong paths, and now may be a good time to reconsider any conclusions you may have reached about recovery being impossible for you. The following chapter continues this journey to explore the different types of trauma.

The following bullet points summarise the main ideas discussed in chapter 11:

- For a long time, CFS has been viewed as a "stress-related illness." I resented that view because I had always seen myself as good at coping with stress—even thriving on it.
- Several therapies were developed to work with the psycho-emotional components of CFS. One of these was Mickel Therapy, which I tried on the advice of my doctor because he had seen it work "miracles" for other patients.
- It turned out that Mickel Therapy was another form of talk therapy focused on making behavioural changes to reduce the body's stress response. I found it interesting, but not the "miracle" I had hoped.
- This left me wondering what could be "wrong" with me. It further underlined my conviction that CFS is not a stress-related illness and led me to reject avenues of exploration that would have been genuinely helpful to my recovery.
- This establishes a common problem: lack of understanding about symptoms can lead to patients being directed towards treatments that aren't right for them or ignoring treatments that could be essential to recovery.
- Trauma is not the "event"; it describes how the individual biology responds to an event. So, it is possible to experience the same event as either a "stress" —opportunity for growth—

or a "trauma"—permanent adaptation of biological processes linked to the Central Nervous System. That same event may even register as "nothing at all" for another person.

- So, when we focus on identifying trauma in terms of events, we are missing the fact that trauma is a biological response that can have far-reaching impacts on many different physiological systems and psycho-emotional behaviours, patterns, and beliefs.
- Trying to identify trauma as an event can also lead people to believe they haven't experienced any trauma simply because they are using a narrow definition of what constitutes a "traumatic event."
- When we explore trauma in the light of a physiological response rather than an event, we can develop a more helpful understanding of how and why a person may be exhibiting symptoms of a maladaptive Central Nervous System.
- This new framework only began coming to light in 1997 in a study into obesity, which became known as the Adverse Childhood Events (ACEs) study. This study identified events that occur in childhood, many of which we would consider to be a "normal" part of growing up, can end up creating biological changes with long-term repercussions for health. These events can end up creating a "signature" that leaves the adult body prone to a variety of diseases, and they can even lead to premature death.
- So, we may need to start addressing the impact of early life events to recover from health issues that appear to have started only in adulthood. In reality, their root causes may lie in our childhood experiences.

- Stress and trauma can both lead to a similar initial response in the Central Nervous System. The difference is that stress is designed to create a growth opportunity—Hormesis, which means your system will naturally re-regulate. The stressful experience will bring you new or enhanced skills—e.g., a stronger immune system, or a greater ability to set and maintain healthy boundaries in a relationship. Trauma occurs when the system becomes overwhelmed and gets stuck in a maladaptive response. So, instead of achieving growth, you may find your body adapts in ways eventually leading to ill health.
- In my experience, Mickel Therapy seemed designed to help with managing ongoing stress. In my opinion, it is not a trauma therapy. So, if your health issues are caused by ongoing stress, it could be helpful, but if your issues are caused by early life trauma, a therapy like Mickel Therapy seems unlikely to address that sufficiently.
- This illustrates the importance of correctly identifying the underlying causes of the physiological and psycho-emotional shifts behind your symptoms. Once correctly identified, you can use a healing modality suited to the specific problem. If you have been using healing modalities not directly related to the root causes of your symptoms, this could be a factor in what is keeping you stuck in the CFS maze.

Your Invitation to Practice

Before we dive into exploring different types of trauma, I invite you to consider how this chapter has changed your view of your body and your CFS experience. You can journal generally or use the following questions as writing prompts:

Before you read this chapter, did you think you were carrying any trauma?

How do you feel now? Do you think your body could be carrying some trauma?

Has any of this information made you think differently about your CFS symptoms?

Out of interest, I invite you to take the basic ACEs questionnaire: how many of the following did you experience while you were under the age of eighteen? Tick all that apply, and count up your total.

- ☐ Did you feel that you didn't have enough to eat, had to wear dirty clothes, or had no one to protect or take care of you?
- ☐ Did you lose a parent through divorce, abandonment, death, or another reason?
- ☐ Did you live with anyone who was depressed or mentally ill or attempted suicide?
- ☐ Did you live with anyone who had a problem with drinking or using drugs, including prescription drugs?
- ☐ Did your parents or adults in your home ever hit, punch, beat, or threaten to harm each other?
- ☐ Did you live with anyone who went to jail or prison?
- ☐ Did a parent or adult in your home ever swear at you, insult you, or put you down?
- ☐ Did a parent or adult in your home ever hit, beat, kick, or physically hurt you in any way?
- ☐ Did you feel that no one in your family loved you or thought you were special?
- ☐ Did you experience unwanted sexual contact?

Notes

Notes

Chapter 12

Identifying Different Types of Trauma

This chapter explores the different types of trauma. This is critical information since different types will have a different impact on your energetic body, and therefore require different modalities to address them. If you are unaware of these differences, it is entirely possible that you have simply been seeking treatment in the wrong area. Without awareness of other options, this may have led you to conclude that your case is hopeless when, in fact, there could be a solution for you. As with any problem in life, if you are not able to identify the root cause of the problem or if you are using the wrong tools to try and carry out a job, the end results are not going to work out very well.

The following bullet points summarise the information shared in chapter 12:

- Childhood Emotional Neglect (CEN) is, sadly, a common fact of life. It doesn't come from unloving or abusive parents. It is simply a reflection of the caregiver's inability to recognize and validate the child's emotions.
- Without recognition and validation, a developing brain learns patterns of behaviour in regard to the emotions. It may learn certain emotions are unacceptable and need to be suppressed. Or it may learn to act out certain emotions in ways that are not productive.
- The patterns become unconscious behaviours in adult life and can trigger the nervous system or be linked to other trauma responses.
- Developmental Trauma relates to a very specific pattern of hard-to-spot trauma because it takes place during a child's early years.
- The work of Laurence Heller, PhD, has identified five critical areas we need to develop if we wish to navigate adult life. These developments take place during the first few years of life and in relation to the way we are treated by primary care-givers.
    - First, Connection. This is the ability to connect to our own body and emotions and the capacity to be in connection with others. Trauma in this area leaves us moving through life feeling disconnected from our bodies and emotions and unable to form meaningful connections with others.
    - Second, Attunement. This is the capacity to attune to our own needs and emotions and to recognize, reach out

for, and receive physical and emotional nourishment from others. Trauma in this area creates difficulty in knowing what we need and beliefs that our needs don't deserve to be met.

- Third, Trust. This leads to the capacity for healthy dependence and interdependence. Trauma in this area can leave us feeling unable to depend on others, so feeling the need to control through power or manipulation.
- Fourth, Autonomy. This means we have the capacity to set appropriate boundaries, say no, and speak our minds without guilt or fear. Trauma in this area creates resentment and difficulty in saying no or setting boundaries.
- Fifth, Love-Sexuality. This is the capacity to live with an open heart and integrate a loving relationship with a vital sexuality. Trauma in this area creates a feeling that self-esteem comes from perfectionism and performance.

- Ancestral Trauma originates in changed gene expression inherited from our ancestors. For example, the grandchildren of Holocaust survivors exhibit gene expression that makes them more susceptible to triggering the nervous system.
- Collective Trauma is linked to Ancestral Trauma but relates more to the Information and awareness of collective memory. For example, tapping into a belief system that sees women—or another minority group—as secondary and deserving of abuse.
- Past-Life Trauma relates to the Karma brought in by the soul when it incarnates into this human body in this life-time.

- PTSD is the most commonly referenced form of Trauma. I define it as a reaction to a specific event, rather than an ongoing lived experience.
- Treatment of PTSD may require different tools and methods for treatment than the other types of trauma discussed in this chapter.
- The reason we would want to identify different trauma types is because they all come together to create the nervous system response that is driving the biological changes creating the symptoms of CFS. By understanding the origins of these, we can move towards using appropriate treatments and tools to address and heal them.
- Although the landscape of trauma is complex, it is not necessary to precisely pinpoint or identify every single traumatic event to heal. Simply becoming aware of triggers and working with them will allow the original unprocessed trauma to come to the surface and become integrated, returning the body to a state of flow and ease.
- This information is not intended to be overwhelming or fear-inducing. It is empowering, giving you a framework for understanding your experience and looking for solutions that will support true healing and recovery from CFS.

Your invitation to practice:

Once more, it is time to reflect upon the information in this chapter. As always, I have offered you some writing prompts in the form of questions. Or, you can simply journal more generally to bring awareness to your developing understanding of trauma.

How do you *feel* about these different trauma types concerning your own personal experience? Do you feel any of them may affect you?

What do you *think* about the information in this chapter? Where do you agree, or disagree, or simply not understand the relevance?

The following questions may help you to identify areas of developmental trauma.[1] Remember, though, we all carry some of this, so identification with the trauma type may or may not have a significant bearing on your symptoms of illness. Please also note how often any of these things apply to you: never/occasionally/most of the time/always.

Connection Trauma Indicators: which of the following apply to you?

- □ Feel terrified and inadequate
- □ Feel shame at existing
- □ Feel like you never fit in
- □ Feel like you are always on the outside looking in
- □ Feel like you're a burden on others
- □ Identify yourself based on your role in life; e.g., I am a mother ... a husband ... a teacher, etc.
- □ See yourself as rational and non-emotional and feel this is a good thing
- □ See yourself as spiritual and above the trappings of "this world"

1 This is not intended to be an official diagnosis of Developmental Trauma. I have put together these questions based on some of the more common ways people with these trauma adaptations identify. If you wish to get a diagnosis, please consult a qualified professional NARM (Neuro-Affective Relational Model) Therapist.

Attunement Trauma Indicators: which of the following apply to you?

- ☐ May be needy
- ☐ Feel unfulfilled and empty
- ☐ Feel like your happiness is dependent on getting something outside of yourself; e.g., the career or relationship or recognition, etc.
- ☐ Feel that you don't have your own needs or don't need others
- ☐ Identify as the giver or helper and enjoy feeling needed by others

Trust Trauma Indicators: which of the following apply to you?

- ☐ Experience difficulty in asking for help directly
- ☐ Feel small and helpless
- ☐ Feel used by others
- ☐ Feel betrayed
- ☐ Feel powerless
- ☐ Feel weak
- ☐ Take pride in being strong and in control
- ☐ See yourself as successful and proud of that
- ☐ Try to be larger than life
- ☐ Betray other people
- ☐ Use or manipulate other people

Autonomy Trauma Indicators: which of the following apply to you?

- ☐ Feel afraid that people won't like you if they really know you
- ☐ Have difficulty expressing any views that you feel could cause conflict
- ☐ Feel angry—even if you don't allow yourself to show it
- ☐ Feel rebellious, but don't necessarily act this out
- ☐ Feel resentful of any type of authority
- ☐ Take enjoyment from behaving in ways that other people don't expect or in disappointing the expectations of others
- ☐ Feel burdened
- ☐ Are always seen as—or try to be—the nice/sweet/compliant person
- ☐ Are the good boy/girl
- ☐ Fear disappointing others
- ☐ Feel proud of being able to take on many things—can carry it all on your shoulders

Love/Sexuality Trauma Indicators: which of the following apply to you?

- ☐ Feel fundamentally flawed or wrong
- ☐ Have constant underlying feelings of hurt
- ☐ Feel rejected
- ☐ Feel unloved and unlovable
- ☐ Are determined you will never let anyone hurt you again
- ☐ Reject others before they have the chance to reject you
- ☐ Self-esteem is based on your appearance and image
- ☐ Desire to be perfect and for everything in life to move seamlessly

Notes

Notes

Chapter 13

Where Is Trauma Stored in Your Body?

This chapter is designed to bring things together from section three of *Finding the Energy to Thrive*. It explores how trauma can translate into a physiological illness. This only makes sense when we see ourselves from the perspective of the "whole person" with the multi-layered Energy body that manifests in a physical body. This is intended to help you connect the dots between the *Four Levels of Creation* model and all the elements it contains, with your physical experience of CFS and the critical role played by trauma. If this picture resonates with you, then it carries the map to recovery. You should be able to use your physical symptoms, your life history, and your ancestral and social heritage as clues to identify where you are carrying trauma. Having made that identification and seeking out appropriate modalities for addressing that trauma, you will eventually experience relief from your physical—

and mental or emotional—symptoms. The next phase of your journey lies in understanding the recovery path. So, we will explore that in the next section.

The following bullet points provide a summary of the information shared in chapter 13:

- Unprocessed emotions are not simply a "theoretical concept"; they are tangible, and we can measure their effects even when we cannot see them.
- From the perspective of your Energy body, your emotions are energetic frequencies. You may be able to sense them in a person's Energy Field—Aura, even if you cannot directly see them.
- They have a visible impact on your physical body, creating observable changes in appearance, hormones, and immune response. Such changes may be observed fleetingly as an emotion flows through—e.g., blushing with shame. Or it may cause a long-term change when an emotion becomes stuck—the science of psycho-neuro-immunology is exploring this.
- All emotions are an Energetic Frequency, and all Energy is in constant flow; it cannot be created or destroyed, but simply change state. So, you cannot "remove" your emotions, but you can cause them to stop flowing freely by creating resistance to experiencing them. This results in inefficient or slow Energy flow in your biofield. So, this is one area in which we "store" unprocessed emotions.
- This then feeds into the physical body. Specifically, muscles and fascia can record the unprocessed trauma emotions, leading to pain and stiffness.

- Polyvagal theory is based on studying the Vagus nerve, which is a major communication system between the brain and body. This nerve assesses both the state of the body and the mind, communicating between the two. So, when you are asked to make a decision, you are not simply calculating in your mind—you are also receiving information from the signals in your body via your Vagus nerve. This can lead to conflict, leaving you confused and uncertain and reducing your capacity for fulfilling social interactions.
- The first metaphor for what trauma stored in the mind/body looks like is a memory bank. This sits in the subconscious mind and is basically all the programs you learned in early life. These programs kept you safe when you first installed them, but they may not have been the wisest behavioural patterns.
- This lack of wisdom may become apparent when, as an adult, you are repeating unhelpful patterns on autopilot and facing challenges as a result.
- The solution is to access the subconscious mind and reprogram the responses that aren't serving you in your current stage of life.
- The second metaphor is the boulder. This represents your core beliefs. Again, these may have their origins in childhood. Like behavioural patterns, we build them up in response to the lessons we learned and the things we observed as we were navigating the world to survive.
- We are not always conscious of our core beliefs. Like boulders, they will suddenly appear in the middle of the road, blocking us from seeing clearly or moving forward with ease.

- Again, as these are held in the subconscious, they tend to come out automatically in reaction to events. And, as we react to these core beliefs, we often find them being reinforced because we are getting the same results that caused us to develop the beliefs in the first place. So, it may feel comforting to hold onto them because they create a sense of security, even if their results are not what we truly desire.
- The next metaphor comes from the saying, "Lock it up and throw away the key." This is dissociation. It relates to the emotions that we have no capacity to process, so rather than remaining in the pain they cause, we find ways to ignore them and avoid seeing them as a part of ourselves: we become fragmented.
- In truth, these parts cannot be eradicated. They need to be processed, which involves feeling the emotion and learning the message it is trying to communicate.
- We may develop very effective adaptations for losing awareness of these parts, but they remain and will always try to come up for release. This is what we are sensing when someone, or something, triggers us. It is rather like that imprisoned part knocking on the door of our conscious mind and asking to be seen and healed.
- The final metaphor is the one that encompasses all of the previous images. Each of those adaptive styles has caused a part of us, a part of our Energy Field, to become frozen and resistant to flow.
- When that happens, your nervous system is sensing the resistance, interpreting this as danger, and signalling this lack of safety to your body. In turn, your cells are responding by

turning on the Cell Danger Response, and physical discomfort results. This may end up with the diagnostic label of CFS.

- All these beautiful, clever adaptations that you developed to keep you safe are resulting in blocked flow, and your physical, mental, and emotional symptoms are simply invitations to process the blocks and open up to an efficient flow.

- In summary, what may look and feel like an inexplicable, frustrating set of symptoms is actually a clever survival adaptation. It developed as the best way to survive in an overwhelming environment. The key word is "survival." For most of us, this is not enough—we desire to thrive.

- In fact, the very essence of our soul is about evolution and growth. It is seeking to understand, overcome, and learn from the challenges we face.

- When we made these intelligent adaptations to survive, they were designed to be temporary—rather like putting off a task you cannot complete in the present moment, but the task doesn't go away.

- As Energy Beings, we operate under the laws of Energy. So, all those unprocessed—trapped or stored—emotions are held at a particular frequency in the Energy Field. They naturally attract energies of the same frequency, not because you are being doomed to a life of misery, but rather as invitations to understand, grow, and heal.

Your Invitation to Practice

It's time to begin exploring your reactions to this chapter. As always, let me provide a framework and invite you to consider the following questions:

What do you *think* about this chapter? Explore your mental reaction to the ideas I have presented.

What do you *feel* about this chapter? Explore your emotional reaction to this material, both as it relates to you, and maybe as it relates to me as well. Perhaps it brings up feelings of shame or confusion towards yourself. Maybe feelings of anger towards me. Hopefully, some more comfortable emotions too—maybe gratitude, hope, and empowerment.

Try an exercise of self-exploration. Can you identify an emotion you try to avoid feeling or expressing? With that emotion in mind, answer the following questions:

Try to think of one to three recent situations that have caused you to feel the emotion.

For each situation, how did you react? Maybe you acted out the emotion, or maybe you suppressed it. Perhaps you engaged in some kind of behaviour to distract yourself from feeling the emotion or addressing the situation. Or did you do something else?

For each situation, how did you feel afterwards? What happened with your physical symptoms? What thoughts went through your mind? What other emotions did you feel? Did you learn any lessons? Did you get any "aha" moments or new revelations? Did this reinforce things you already believe about yourself, the other people involved, or the world around you?

Would you have liked to do something differently? If so, what? How might that have looked and felt to you?

Notes

Chapter 14

Treatment Options

Having put together a model of the potential root causes of CFS, the next logical question is: What do you do about them? So, this chapter explores treatment options. It is not designed to evaluate each individual treatment or recommend any specific treatment but to provide a model to help you understand the pros and cons of different options. Treatment options are changing constantly as researchers and practitioners develop new ideas or find new ways of using older ideas. So, analysing the current options would only provide information that is quickly out of date. It is more helpful to understand what *type* of treatment is required for different symptom sets than to understand which treatments fall into that *type*. This model should also allow you to map new treatments in the future. Within this model, it is also important to understand that you are working with a complex illness.

So, it is rare for a single treatment to provide all the answers. What you will need to do is take your personal list of symptoms and map them to the treatment types to build a plan. I am not suggesting that you self-diagnose and self-treat; you may need to build this plan with the help of one or more qualified professionals who really understand CFS. Although there will be areas where you can help yourself, you will certainly need to call upon professional help at some point. So, the process of creating your treatment plan may also need to consider things like your ability to travel for treatment or your budget. These are areas that we will explore further in the following two chapters.

The following bullet points summarise the ideas shared in chapter 14:

- The place for you to begin is by identifying whether you need to recover from PTSD or Developmental Trauma—or both.
- The tools for treating these types of trauma are different. PTSD relates to a single life-threatening event, and it is linked to an external trigger—or triggers. It can be treated successfully. EMDR has a particularly good track record for this type of trauma.
- Developmental Trauma occurs as a result of ongoing deficits in your relations with key caregivers in early life. It creates a pain-body held in your Energy field, and the trigger for this type of trauma is you! You will be living day to day with emotions like powerlessness, worthlessness, self-hatred, and survival fear, and you may not even be consciously aware of this if you have never known anything else. Survival fear is living with the belief that you might be about to die at any second. This creates a constant elevation of the nervous system, and even the smallest task which you otherwise might take for granted (e.g. walking out of your house) can trigger awareness of all

the ways in which you might face death when you take that action. Survivor's guilt comes specifically from surviving an actual experience of death, particularly when others around you died, and you wonder why you were "chosen" to live. You feel the pain and loss experienced by other people and deem this to be unfair: you feel guilty that others are experiencing pain and you/your loved ones were spared that pain.

- Addressing this type of trauma requires tools that work with frequency and resonance for day-to-day management and with Geometry or Information if you are seeking full recovery.
- The tools of frequency and resonance work on the principles of physics. The types of emotions held in the pain-body vibrate at a low frequency. If you can expose them to high frequency, they will shatter. It is the same principle as an opera singer hitting a high note and shattering a glass. Developmental Trauma essentially stems from the lack of unconditional love. Exposure to unconditional love—from within yourself—can heal this type of trauma. That is the principle.
- In practice, effective modalities include NARM Therapy—NeuroAffective Relational Model, EFT—Emotional Freedom Technique, EMDR—Eye Movement Desensitisation and Reprocessing, Sound Therapy, Bioenergetics, NLP—Neuro Linguistic Programming, and more.
- Where people can end up "going wrong" is in underestimating the amount of time it takes to heal Developmental Trauma. So, it is important—at least helpful—to find a practice that you can also carry out in your own time at home.
- Dr Bruce Lipton's research indicates that 95% of our genes can be switched on and off in response to our environment. Part of that environment comprises the pain-body resulting

from Developmental Trauma. So, working in this area can create beneficial changes in your epigenetic expression as well.

- To derive benefit from any sort of treatment, your body needs a basic level of energy to support it. That foundation is laid by focusing on your physical environment—what I call the "basic pillars of health."
- This includes nutrition and adequate water, light, air, and movement. You can create this foundation through lifestyle changes that are free to implement. If you need more details about how to do that, please visit my website, https://www.findmyenergy.co.uk/the-basic-environment-for-healing-and-supporting-cfs/
- At some point, you are likely to need more targeted support from a trained nutritionist who can assess your specific needs. This will save you money in the long run, as you won't be wasting funds on supplements that don't support your body.
- No single treatment is "better" or "worse." It very much depends on your personal needs.
- Some treatments have undergone more research than others. That doesn't mean they are necessarily "better" —just better researched.
- Each of us is different, so it is hard to be guided by what works for others. Something may work for you and not others, or vice versa.
- When you are researching different options, try to tap into your intuition as well as your logical mind. So, how is your body responding to reading about this type of treatment? Do you feel drawn to it? Does it feel good to you as well as make logical sense?

- Research into the Placebo and Nocebo effects has demonstrated that our minds have the power to create physiological changes in our bodies.
- Believing that a treatment will—or won't—be effective for you can create powerful impacts on the outcome of the treatment.
- The practitioner offering the treatment can also create a placebo or nocebo effect in you. For example, do you trust them and feel they understand your situation and understand the illness?
- Understanding this potential can empower you to support the efficacy of any treatment, through what you believe it to be capable of doing. It can also explain why certain treatments may not work. If your existing trauma is creating mental blocks to healing, addressing those specific blocks may be a necessary foundation for you.

Your Invitation to Practice

As usual, I would like to invite you to journal about your response to the information you've just learned in this chapter. What do you think about it? What emotions has it raised in you?

In addition to that "normal" practice, I invite you to start on a slightly longer-term project. I would like you to begin creating a list of possible treatment avenues. This is going to become ongoing research you can use to begin guiding yourself towards creating a personalised program to address your needs. So, you can start by working through the following questions:

What treatments for CFS have you tried in the past or are you undertaking now? List each one.

Against each of those listed, please answer the following questions:

Has this treatment been effective for you?

Based on what you have been learning in this chapter and earlier in the book, why do you think that might be? I mean, why was it effective if you derived benefit, or why wasn't it effective if you didn't derive benefit?

Let's look at your expectations about this treatment. Often, our assessment of the benefit of a treatment is coloured by our expectations of what it would bring us. Were you expecting the treatment to give you a complete cure? If so, then in what timeframe did you expect that to take place? If not, were you expecting the treatment to deal with a specific symptom, or set of symptoms, and did it do that?

Now, I would like you to make a list of treatments that you haven't yet tried. Start with the treatments listed in this chapter. Add in any others that you have come across as being either recommended for CFS specifically or for trauma more generally.

Over time, I want you to begin researching each of those treatments. For each one, answer the following questions as best you can:

Does the treatment—logically—sound like it could help you, based on your understanding of your own symptoms and experience?

Do you feel drawn to the treatment?

What is preventing you from signing up for this treatment right away?

Notes

Chapter 15

Getting Realistic About the Recovery Process

The purpose of this chapter is to help you avoid the most common pitfalls that prevent people from accessing full recovery. Although I am not promising any specific outcome for anybody, I know enough people who have experienced recovery that I am willing to suggest that I believe it is possible. We have already explored some of the blocks to experiencing recovery. Those might include things like lack of awareness, which leads to misidentifying what symptoms mean or using inappropriate treatments. However, even if you have correctly understood the messages your body is trying to communicate, and you are following helpful protocols to support recovery, there are a few common mistakes that can still hinder you. These largely relate to expectations and mindset. They are all completely accidental and result from a lack of awareness. So, the material in this chapter will help you become aware of any patterns that might have hindered you in the past or present. Now, if you do notice any of these patterns, it is OK: Once you see them, you can change them. So, this information should bring you even more cause for hope. If you are just starting your recovery journey, then you can begin with the awareness of the most common pitfalls so that you can see and avoid them before they impact you.

The following bullet points summarise the ideas and information shared in chapter 15:

- We tend to have a preconceived idea about what it feels like to recover from an illness. That idea often comes from a much simpler type of illness—for example, a common virus like influenza.
- Recovery from a chronic complex illness like CFS is altogether different. It does not follow a smooth linear path. Instead, it will feel like a rollercoaster of improvements and setbacks.
- This is because you are working through multiple layers, rather like peeling an onion. So, each layer will be moving you forwards, but it may not always feel like that.
- One of the main reasons people remain stuck in CFS is because they don't understand that idea. So, when the recovery path gets bumpy or seems too slow, they interpret that to mean that recovery isn't possible for them, and they just give up. In reality, the final layer might be the next one you remove, but you won't discover this if you lose faith and stop too soon.
- The recovery process will require you to layer up protocols or treatments. So, don't make the mistake of doing some

nutrition work, recognising you haven't recovered, and then stopping the nutrition to try something else instead. You need to maintain the nutritional foundation and then add the next benefit on top. It's rather like building a house: you need foundations AND walls AND a roof, not just some of those elements.

- You also need to make sure that all parts of you are in alignment. If you are providing your cells with great nutritional support through supplements, for example, but your nervous system is still running a trauma pattern, your cells will be receiving mixed messages. The physical support is prompting them to maximise their energy. The nervous system is signalling it is unsafe to operate fully in the world. So, you need to address both issues and bring everything into alignment so your cells get one clear, congruent message.
- This section is about getting real with you. The way in which we experience life has a lot to do with our expectations. So, if you set expectations and the reality doesn't match up, you may experience disappointment. This is another common pitfall on the CFS recovery path. You have a set of expectations that don't materialise, so you turn that into a story that tells you CFS is for life and recovery is impossible.
- Secondly, get real about the idea of setting intentions. I'm sure you do intend to recover. And that intention is necessary and powerful. Yet don't get sucked into the idea it is enough all by itself. Your intention needs to be backed up by concrete, consistent action.
- The recovery path is rather like running a marathon. I have been using these pages to share my experience with the intention of being a good friend to you. Some of the messages

I have shared may not be what you wish to hear, but hearing the truth, however undesirable, is going to support you far better than someone telling you what you wish to hear. Like a real marathon, recovery is a process. It has challenges, and there will be times when you question yourself, your choices, and even your desire to recover. But I can also testify that the euphoria of making it out of your maze and opening up all the possibilities of life is well worth all the challenges and doubts.

- Lastly, there is no obligation to recover. You may simply desire to reach a place of greater comfort and rest there—and that's OK. You choose how far you go and what you are willing to experience. To facilitate that process, you really want to learn how to cultivate acceptance of where you are right now, each and every day. Remember, you may not have much choice over the level of pain, but you have complete choice over how much you suffer with that pain.
- Finally, it is important to spend a little time contemplating how you will know that you have recovered. What exactly will your life look and feel like when you have recovered from CFS? Are those expectations realistic? If you are expecting never to get tired again, never to catch another virus, and suddenly to be running marathons, that may be unrealistic. You may be chasing a rainbow that is really about future growth, not just basic recovery.
- You also need to recognise that the process of moving from "basically recovered" back into "normal life" requires some conscious attention. Even though your cells may now be functioning optimally, long periods of physical debilitation may mean that you need to do some basic body reconditioning. Some people also need to address some PTSD attached to having the illness. You can end up being triggered by perfectly

"normal" symptoms, and those triggers cause a psycho-emotional response that appears to manifest a physical relapse. If that is happening, it is important to recognise this is an issue to address through psycho-emotional support.

- The final stages of recovery are still a time when you need to show yourself a great deal of self-compassion. Even if you do recognise yourself responding with emotions that you would rather not face, know that these responses are coming from patterns that have kept you alive in the past. You are not faulty, or shameful, or to blame: the re-appearance of these emotions or patterns is simply their way of asking to be let go because you are moving on to greater things than you could possibly have imagined.

Your Invitation to Practice

For this invitation to practice, I would like to invite you to complete the following set of questions. You can also journal about this chapter and what you have learned from it if you wish. Most importantly, let's bring some awareness to any misconceptions you have about what your recovery journey will look and feel like. That will empower you to avoid the common mistakes that keep people stuck in chronic fatigue.

What do you expect your life to look and feel like when you have recovered? In detail ... what job or other activity will you be doing? What will your social life look like? How about your family structure? When you have outlined all of that, do a sanity check ... are all of these things really about recovery, or are you perhaps confusing some with growth steps that you want to go on and take after your recovery has stabilised?

If you have already been following a recovery path, look back at your experience. Have there been times when you did any of the following?

Abandoned one type of treatment and replaced it with another—If so, do you feel that was wise, or had you slipped into the trap of making substitutions when you might have derived greater benefit from layering up new support?

Experienced a recurrence of symptoms and interpreted that as a sign that things were going wrong—Is this really what was happening, or was your body trying to eradicate something that has been weighing it down, and it wants to let go?

Fallen into patterns of despair or given up hope because you haven't recovered to the degree that you expected in the time you hoped—Was this really a sign that you can't recover, or were your expectations a little unrealistic?

What wise and compassionate learnings can you take to move forward and support yourself now?

Notes

Notes

Chapter 16

Overcoming Roadblocks on the Recovery Path

Having explored expectations in the last chapter, this important final chapter looks at the two most common roadblocks on the recovery path. In some cases, these blocks are real, but often they simply seem like dead ends even though they can be overcome. Finally, this chapter addresses the last important piece of the puzzle. What if you don't recover? I intend that my story and discoveries will provide you with hope and a real path out of your CFS maze. At the same time, I spent many years stuck in that maze, and I know the search for recovery takes its toll on you in different ways; trying to walk the tightrope of hope and despair is tricky. At times, my only solution was to find acceptance of my situation. In those moments, the last thing I wanted to hear or read was another hopeful recovery story that seemed to underline my own personal failure, which is how I perceived it. So, I wish to end with some words of comfort for those of you who feel like the CFS maze is going to be your permanent place of residence for this lifetime. Whatever the end point of your journey, know that you are loved, that you are worthy, and that you are brave for waking up each day and accepting your current reality.

The following bullet points offer a quick summary of the larger ideas covered in chapter 16:

- Are you someone who has heard about or explored, treatments in the past and decided not to pursue them simply because you felt you couldn't afford the price?
- This can be a legitimate reason. And it can also be something masking some deeper issues relating to your beliefs about your own self-worth and money.
- Money is just energy. That means it is simply a tool to empower us to enjoy things we desire or need. It also means it is in constant flow. Yet, we are often brought up with beliefs about whether it's "good" to spend money on certain things or that money is scarce and finite. Those beliefs can be examined, addressed, and potentially overcome if you desire.
- So, ask yourself this: If you come across a treatment or practitioner that you believe can help you, would you view that as a "cost" or an "investment" in your future? And if you choose not to take the opportunity to get help, what is the cost of making that choice? How will your life look five or ten years from now? Is that a choice you really wish to make? Spoiler alert! There isn't a "right" or "wrong" answer to those questions.

- This second roadblock can feel triggering because it taps into some of the grossly unfair ideas that the general population has come to believe about CFS. The illness is not something created by the person living with it, and it is not a matter of conscious choice to live with or recover from CFS.
- At the same time, the unconscious mind can inadvertently end up influencing the course of recovery. There may be parts of the unconscious that view some of the practical implications of CFS as being beneficial. For example, if you are someone who prefers to be quiet and unseen, CFS achieves that result beautifully. There is a way to recover and honour the needs of the subconscious mind, which are only ever trying to protect you.
- Unconscious blocks can accidentally create nocebo effects, which mean that even beneficial treatments don't work. So, if you are going round in circles, it is worth at least considering whether there are any parts of you that benefit in any way from living with CFS and whether they can enjoy the same benefits within a life in which you are free from pain and feel energised.
- I wish to end by reminding you that everything is a choice, whether you make that choice consciously or unconsciously. I know you are making the perfect choice for you.
- Living with CFS doesn't have to be "bad." We do not have to pathologize the illness. If you can find a level of acceptance in which your experience allows you to enjoy life as much as you desire, that is wonderful.
- So, this book is not about forcing anyone to follow any particular path. It is here to open your eyes to different ideas and allow you to continue making your choices, trusting they are right for you and making them from a more conscious perspective.

Your Invitation to Practice

For the final time, I invite you to reflect on the information shared here and answer the following questions:

What are your beliefs around finances? Write down some memes that come to mind for you. Write down the values around spending and saving that your parents taught you. Add in any other beliefs you have gained through your adult life, and make a note of how and why you came to believe these things.

How do you feel about spending money on yourself? Write down where these beliefs came from—your own experience or things that other people have told you or shown you.

How do you see money? In particular, think about your views on scarcity and flow.

How do you look at the price of a treatment: as a cost or as an investment?

What would you need to know or understand in order to be willing to pay for a treatment? As you consider this, do you feel your expectation is realistic?

Do you believe that your mindset can control how you feel physically, and why do you believe this? Your belief could come from your personal experience or from things other people have told you.

Revisit the notes you made in the practice at the end of chapter 7 and see if you can identify any secondary gains. How do these benefits serve you? Is there another way in which you could attain the same benefit? You can let your imagination fly there—anything can be possible.

How do you think and feel about the information in this chapter? What learnings can you take forward and apply to your own circumstances?

Notes

Conclusion

Exiting Your Maze

Finding the Energy to Thrive concludes by offering you an outline of the five steps to recovery, which will support you in arranging your journaled observations into a way out of your CFS maze. So, if you need that, please go and read the book. If you would like to continue travelling with me as your guide, I will tell you a little about the support I am able to offer you.

As I was completing my own recovery journey, I began to intuitively develop a practice to support myself. The practice involved using colour cards to help me see and explore the issues that were arising for me each day. I then spent time relaxing and reflecting whilst colouring Mandalas and other shapes. I would journal about my experiences and any revelations that had occurred during my reflection, and this allowed me to reintegrate all those "lost" parts that were depleting my energy while they waited to be seen and accepted. I learned that the process of reintegration doesn't need to involve any fancy techniques. It really is as simple as being able to witness and accept my inner world, learn any lessons and simply allow my body to heal. The more I was able to find peace and acceptance, the more pieces came forth and reintegrated. This was an incredibly powerful, yet gentle process. I was guiding my own pace of recovery and intuitively supporting myself. Yes, I had already built a physical foundation by creating a supportive lifestyle that focused on good nutrition, sleep, and pacing my activities, so my physical body was receiving the support it required. My reflective practice then became a means of supporting the process of recovery in my Energy body.

Each practice became a mirror for seeing patterns from my past that were still manifesting in my present, and learning the lessons that they were here to offer. Each time I completed a mandala, I was creating a work of art that was unique: a personal reflection of me. As I looked at those works of art, I began to see my own perfection[2] and appreciate my worth, and I truly began to love and accept myself. All very naturally and gently, using a process that felt almost like a "game," an invitation for my inner children to step forth and play in safety and feel seen and loved. So, although I had worked with many healing modalities, I was discovering that my own innate, intuitive abilities provided the final route out of my CFS maze.

I had never anticipated developing any kind of modality or system, yet I felt compelled to develop this into something that other people could try. As I began to show my art to friends and family and describe what I was doing, they became interested and wished to try this as well. All found the process gentle and deeply connecting. So, this felt like something to be shared more widely. It has developed into the Kolorlan System.

I created my own set of colour cards, using principles that relate to the *Four Levels of Creation* model. I stopped colouring other people's mandalas and began creating my own, using the ideas that underpin Sacred Geometry.[3] You may have heard mention of Sacred Geometry and assumed it was "just" a cute-sounding name for something intended to "cheat" you into believing it has some power when it has no real meaning. In fact, nothing could be further from the truth. The shapes found in Sacred Geometry represent the Information found

---

2 We are all perfect in the present moment in all our perceived "imperfections."

3 In case you are wondering about qualifications, I completed much rigourous study and gained a Diploma in Colour Therapy to support that side of the system. I studied the biofield and qualified as a certified Bioenergetic Health Coach, and I have also followed courses in trauma therapy, Neuro-Linguistic Programming, and life coaching and begun studying the scientific and metaphysical principles of Sacred Geometry.

in the Universal and human biofields. This is the Information that shapes your blueprint, the Information that can become distorted and lead to the physical manifestation of challenges in all shapes and sizes, as we explored in the *Intuitive Level* of the *Four Levels of Creation* model. Dr Robert Gilbert[4] speaks of it as "the thought-forms of God," and the science of Cymatics demonstrates how those shapes manifest through sound frequency to become a visible pattern in the physical world. Dr Ibrahim Karim has carried out magnificent research to begin decoding some of the geometry and using it to support physical healing in people, improvements in agriculture, and protection from EMFs in the environment.[5] This work is still in its infancy, and I am not making any bold claims of my own, but the concept of Sacred Geometry is far more powerful than most people realise.

The Kolorlan System offers you the opportunity to support yourself through absorbing the frequencies of colour and Sacred Geometry shapes whilst gently exploring your inner world and integrating whatever is ready to be seen. You can use it to support the journaling practices in this book or to reflect on any other area of your life. It is fun, relaxing, and inexpensive and can be adapted to suit your lifestyle. You aren't required to travel or work with any practitioner, and you can do as much or as little as your energy levels permit. So, if you would like to discover the magic that this can unfold for you, please visit: https://findmyenergy.co.uk/kolorlan-system.

---

4 Dr Robert Gilbert offers courses in Sacred Geometry at https://vesica.org

5 You can learn more about this work in Dr Karim's book, *Biogeometry Signatures: Harmonizing the Body's Subtle Energy Exchange with the Environment*

Printed in Great Britain
by Amazon

62875392R00107